LEARN TO
Fair Isle
CROCHET™

Contents

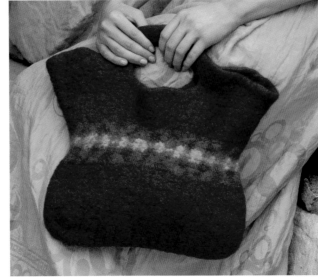

INTRODUCTION

"Fair Isle is a traditional knitting technique used to create patterns with multiple colors. It is named after Fair Isle, a tiny island in the north of Scotland, between the Orkney and Shetland islands. Fair Isle knitting gained considerable popularity when the Prince of Wales (later to become Edward VIII) wore Fair Isle tank tops in public in 1921. Traditional Fair Isle patterns have a limited palette of five or so colors, use only two colors per row, are worked in the round and limit the length of a run of any particular color.

"Some people use the term 'Fair Isle' to refer to any colorwork knitting where stitches are knit alternately in various colors, with the unused colors stranded across the back of the work. Others use the term 'stranded colorwork' for the generic technique, and reserve the term 'Fair Isle' for the characteristic patterns of the Shetland Islands."
—*Taken from Wikipedia*

As a child, I fell in love with Fair Isle sweaters. They were a staple in my wardrobe. I loved the colors and the patterns. And as a crocheter, I always wanted to make them.

It took me 30 years to learn to knit, and when I did, I poured over knitting books that taught Fair Isle. It was then I discovered that I could have done this all along! And now I can share it with all of you.

Many crocheters think that Fair Isle is just another form of intarsia or tapestry crochet. What most crocheters don't realize is that Fair Isle actually refers to the patterns that are used. In knitting, Fair Isle work must be stranded because unlike crochet, there really isn't a way to work over the unused yarn. But in crochet, you can carry the yarn behind to strand like traditional Fair Isle or you work over the yarn as you would in intarsia. Whichever way you want to learn to work this technique, I hope you enjoy crocheted Fair Isle as much as I!

TIPS TO GET STARTED

Fair Isle crochet has long been compared to "tapestry crochet" or even intarsia. However, I find that though it can be done both ways, working in a "stranded colorwork" style gives a beautiful look. The fabric is less bulky; when using colors that are very different, you will notice that the darker color does not show through the lighter color.

One of the keys to making Fair Isle crochet look like its knitted counterpart is to always work on the right side of the work. This means either working in the round or, in the case of flat pieces such as afghans, working on the right side only. In the second case, you will have ends to weave in, use as fringe or there are ways to crochet the ends into an edging that will hide them.

Another discovery I have made in developing this technique is that the "pattern" or "image(s)" show up more clearly in the fabric if you work in the **back loop of the single crochet** (*see Stitch Guide*). The ridge that forms helps define each stitch and the pattern "pops." You also will find that the ridge gives the illusion of the stitches being right on top of each other and not "leaning"—therefore the image is not distorted as normal intarsia crochet can be.

READING A CHART

Reading a Fair Isle chart is easy! All you have to remember is that one square = one single crochet. The color of the square tells you what color yarn to use.

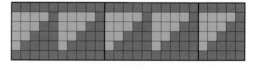

Chart A

COLOR KEY
■ A
■ B

Also, if you are right-handed, you read every row from right to left.

If you are left-handed, read every row from left to right. It's that simple!

HOW TO DO A BASIC FLAT FAIR ISLE SAMPLER—STRANDING

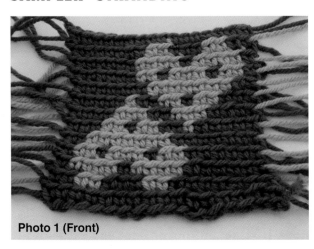

Photo 1 (Front)

Photo 2 (Back)

In the following pattern, only 2 colors are used.

INSTRUCTIONS
Note: When starting and ending each row, leave a 4-inch end at both ends. Carry colors not in use on WS of work.

Ch 16. Fasten off.

Row 1: Make slip knot on hook and join yarn with sc in first ch, sc in each ch across. Fasten off. *(16 sc)*

Row 2: Make slip knot on hook and working in back lps, join yarn with sc in first sc, sc in each rem sc across. Fasten off.

Rows 3–13: Follow Chart B and tips to complete the pattern.

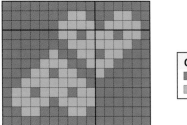

COLOR KEY
■ A
■ B

Chart B

SOME TIPS TO REMEMBER WHILE CREATING THE STRANDED FABRIC
When starting each row, work OVER the 2nd color of the row in the first stitch. Carry color(s) not in use on wrong side of work until needed.

Front of work with carry color.

Back of work with carry color.

When switching colors in the row, be sure to change color in the last stitch of previous color by completing stitch with the new color.

Photo 5

Completing the color change.

On the wrong side, when switching colors, make sure to "twist" the 2 colors so that a hole will not form.

Photo 6

Back of work twisting colors.

HOW TO DO A BASIC FLAT FAIR ISLE SAMPLER—WORKING OVER YARN

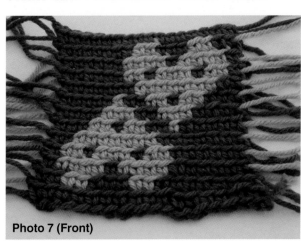

Photo 7 (Front)

Photo 8 (Back)

INSTRUCTIONS

Note: When starting and ending each row, leave a 4-inch end at both ends. Work over color(s) not in use.

Ch 16. Fasten off.

Row 1: Make slip knot on hook and join yarn with sc in first ch, sc in each ch across. Fasten off. *(16 sc)*

Row 2: Make slip knot on hook and working in back lps, join yarn with sc in first sc, sc in each rem sc across. Fasten off.

Rows 3–13: Follow Chart B and tips below to complete the pattern.

SOME TIPS TO REMEMBER WHILE CREATING THE FABRIC

When starting each row, work OVER the 2nd color of the row in the first stitch REGARDLESS of the color and work over 2nd color.

Photo 9

Front of work with carry color.

Back of work with carry color.

When switching colors on the row, be sure to change color in the last stitch of previous color by completing stitch with the new color (*see Photo 5 on page 4*).

On the wrong side, when working over the unused color, be sure to hold that color taut so that it doesn't come through the stitch completely.

Completed carried row.

FINISHING BORDER
FRONT CASING

Rnd 1: With RS facing, beg in upper right corner and working in **front lps** (*see Stitch Guide and Photo 12*), join yarn with sc in first sc, 2 sc in same sc, sc in each sc across to last st, 3 sc in last sc, working across next side in ends of rows, sc in end of each row using one strand of yarn at edge of row (*see photo 13*), working across next side in chs of foundation ch and in front lps, 3 sc in first ch, sc in each ch to last ch, 3 sc in last ch, working across next side in ends of rows, sc in each row using one strand of yarn at edge of row, join with sl st in first sc (*see photo 14*).

Working in front loops.

Working in ends of rows.

Rnd 1 completed.

Rnd 2: Ch 1, sc in each sc around, working 3 sc in 2nd sc of each 3-sc group.

Rnd 3: Rep rnd 2. Fasten off.

Note: Additional rnds may be worked for a wider border.

BACK CASING

Rnd 1: With WS facing, beg in upper right corner and working in front lps *(see photo 15)*, join yarn with sc in first sc, sc in each sc across to last st, 3 sc in last sc, working across next side in ends of rows, sc in end of each row using one strand of yarn at edge of row *(see photo 16)*, working across next side in chs of foundation ch and in front lps, 3 sc in first ch, sc in each ch to last ch, 3 sc in last ch, working across next side in ends of rows, sc in each row using one strand of yarn at edge of row, join with sl st in first sc *(see photo 17)*.

Rnd 2: Ch 1, sc in each sc around, working 3 sc in 2nd sc of each 3-sc group.

Rnd 3: Rep rnd 2.

Photo 18

Completed casing on both sides of fabric.

Photo 15

Working in front loops on back side.

CLOSING CASING

Working through both Front Casing and Back Casing, sc in each sc around *(see photo 19)*, having ends left on either side of piece tucked into casing before closing.

Note: *Ends may be cut shorter to reduce bulk in casing.*

Photo 19

Working through both casings.

Photo 16

Working on ends of rows on back side.

Photo 17

Completed Rnd 1 on back side.

Photo 20

Completed casing.

HOW TO DO A BASIC IN THE ROUND FAIR ISLE SAMPLER

In this section we are going to work a simple pattern of 6 rounds using a simple pattern. Choose to work the yarn either stranded or not.

Rnd 1: Ch 26, sc in 2nd ch from hook, sc in each rem ch across. *(25 sc)*

Photo 22

Completed piece.

Photo 21

Rnd 1 completed.

Note: Follow Chart A and tips to complete pattern.

Rnds 2–6: Sc in each sc around. At end of last rnd, fasten off *(see photo 22)*.

TIPS FOR WORKING IN THE ROUND

Do not pull yarn not in use too tightly. There should be some stretch in the fabric.

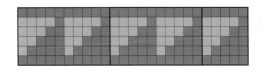

Chart A

COLOR KEY
■ A
■ B

Do not join rounds or work a beginning chain as this will distort the pattern.

Use a stitch marker to mark first stitch of round.

At the end of the last round, join with a slip stitch to first stitch. Fasten off. ■

Fingerless Mitts & Leggins

FINGERLESS MITTS

SKILL LEVEL

EASY

FINISHED SIZE
Fits 8–9½-inch wrist and hand circumference

MATERIALS
- Cascade Yarns Fixation light (DK) weight cotton/elastic yarn (100 yds/ 50g per skein):
  3 skeins each #3611 red, #8990 black, #8797 gray and #8176 off-white
- Size G/6/4mm crochet hook or size needed to obtain gauge
- Tapestry needle
- Stitch marker

GAUGE
4 sc and 4 sc rows = 1 inch

Take time to check gauge.

PATTERN NOTES
Weave in ends as work progresses.

Join with slip stitch as indicated unless otherwise stated.

Every row is worked on right side.

Work in continuous rounds for first 18 rounds, work in rows for next 4 rows, and work in continuous rounds for last 14 rounds. The unjoined rows form thumb opening.

Leave a 6-inch end when fastening off yarn.

Each row/round is worked carrying unused color across wrong side. Solid color rows/rounds have a 2nd strand of same color carried on wrong side.

If you are right-handed, read every row of chart from right to left.

If you are left-handed, read every row of chart from left to right.

MITT
MAKE 2.

Rnd 1: With red, ch 36 loosely, **join** *(see Pattern Notes)* in first ch to form a ring, ch 1, **carrying a strand of red on WS** *(see Pattern Notes)* and working in **back lps** *(see Stitch Guide)* sc in each ch around, do not join. *(36 sc)*

Note: Place st marker in first st of rnd, moving up as work progresses. For following rnds, follow chart for color changes and work in back lps.

Rnds 2–18: Sc in each sc around. At end of last rnd, fasten off.

Note: For following rows, follow chart for color changes and work in back lps.

Row 19: Now working in rows, make slip knot on hook and join yarn with sc in back lp of first sc, sc in each rem sc across. Fasten off.

Row 20: Make slip knot on hook and join yarn in back lp of first sc, sc in each rem sc across. Fasten off.

Rows 21 & 22: Rep row 20.

Note: Remainder of Mitt is worked in rnds. Place st marker in first st of rnd, moving up as work progresses. For following rnds, follow chart for color changes and work in back lps.

Rnds 23–36: Sc in each sc around. At end of last rnd, fasten off.

FINISHING

Join red in bottom of thumb opening, ch 1, sc evenly sp around opening, join in beg sc. Fasten off.

LEGGINS

SKILL LEVEL

EASY

SIZES

Instructions given fit size small; changes for size large are in [ ].

FINISHED SIZE

Circumference: 9 inches *(small)* [12 inches *(large)*]
Length: 24 inches

MATERIALS

- Cascade Yarns Fixation light (DK) weight cotton/elastic yarn (100 yds/ 50g per skein):
    3 skeins each #3611 red, #8990 black, #8797 gray and #8176 off-white
- Size G/6/4mm crochet hook or size needed to obtain gauge
- Tapestry needle
- Stitch marker

GAUGE

4 sc and 4 sc rows = 1 inch

Take time to check gauge.

PATTERN NOTES

Weave in ends as work progresses.

Join with slip stitch as indicated unless otherwise stated.

Leggins are worked in continuous rounds. Do not join unless specified; mark beginning of round.

Leave a 6-inch end when fastening off yarn.

Each round is worked carrying unused color across wrong side. Solid color rounds have a 2nd strand of same color carried on wrong side.

If you are right-handed, read every row of chart from right to left.

If you are left-handed, read every row of chart from left to right.

LEGGIN
MAKE 2.

Rnd 1: With red, ch 48 [60] loosely, **join** *(see Pattern Notes)* in first ch to form a ring, ch 1, **carrying a strand of red underneath** *(see Pattern Notes)*, working in **back lps** *(see Stitch Guide)* sc in each ch across, do not join. *(48 [60] sc)*

Note: Place st marker in first st of rnd, moving up as work progresses. For following rnds, follow chart for color changes.

Rnds 2–72: Working in back lps, sc in each sc around. At end of last rnd, fasten off.

RIBBING

Row 1: Join black in any sc on rnd 72, ch 13, sc in 2nd ch from hook, sc in each ch across, sl st in each of next 2 sc on rnd 72, turn. *(12 sc)*

Row 2: Ch 1, working in back lps, sc in each sc across, turn.

Row 3: Ch 1, working in back lps, sc in each sc across, sl st in each of next 2 sc on rnd 72, turn.

Rep rows 2 and 3 in rem sc on rnd 72. At end of last row, fasten off.

Rep on opposite end of Leggin working in chs of foundation ch.

FINISHING

Sew ends of ribbing together. ∎

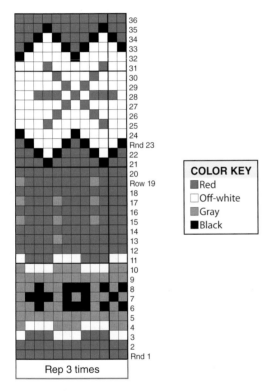

Fingerless Mitts
Chart

COLOR KEY
- ■ Red
- □ Off-white
- ▨ Gray
- ■ Black

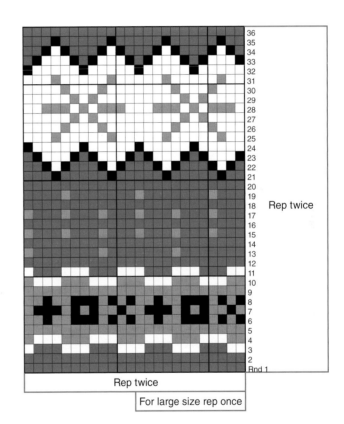

Leggins
Chart

Cowl

SKILL LEVEL

EASY

SIZE
One size

FINISHED SIZE
13½ inches wide x 34 inches in circumference

MATERIALS
- Universal Yarn Deluxe Chunky bulky (chunky) weight yarn (3½ oz/ 120 yds/100g per skein):
  1 skein each #3711 madder red, #1900 ebony and #91879 natural
- Universal Yarn Classic Chunky bulky (chunky) weight yarn (3½ oz/131 yds/ 100g per skein):
  1 skein #60726 ocean wave
- Size J/10/6mm crochet hook or size needed to obtain gauge
- Tapestry needle
- Stitch marker

GAUGE
16 sc = 5½ inches; 9½ sc rows = 4 inches

Take time to check gauge.

PATTERN NOTES
Weave in ends as work progresses.

Join with slip stitch as indicated unless otherwise stated.

Cowl is worked in continuous rounds. Do not join unless specified; mark beginning of rounds.

Leave a 6-inch end when fastening off yarn.

Each round is worked carrying unused color across wrong side. Solid color rounds have a 2nd strand of same color carried on wrong side.

If you are right-handed, read every row of chart from right to left.

If you are left-handed, read every row of chart from left to right.

COWL
Rnd 1: With madder red, ch 96 loosely, **join** (see *Pattern Notes*) in first ch to form a ring, ch 1, **carrying a strand of bittersweet on WS** (*see Pattern Notes*) and working in **back lps** (*see Stitch Guide*), sc in each ch across. Do not join. (*96 sc*)

Note: Place st marker in first st of rnd, moving up as work progresses. For following rnds, follow chart for color changes and work in back lps.

Rnds 2–31: Sc in each sc around. At end of last rnd, fasten off. ∎

COLOR KEY
- ■ Madder red
- ■ Ebony
- □ Natural
- ■ Ocean wave

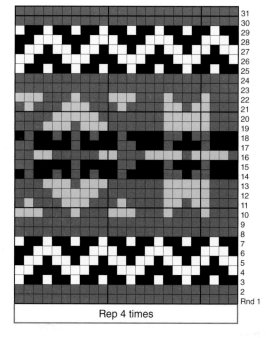

Rep 4 times

Cowl
Chart

Shawl

SKILL LEVEL

EASY

FINISHED SIZE
13 inches wide x 75 inches long

MATERIALS
- Universal Yarn Deluxe Worsted medium (worsted) weight yarn (3½ oz/220 yds/100g per skein):
  - 6 skeins #3669 Caribbean sea
  - 1 skein each #91476 fire red, #41795 nectarine, #12270 natural and #71006 white ash
- Size G/6/4mm crochet hook or size needed to obtain gauge
- Tapestry needle
- Stitch marker

GAUGE
14 sc and 16 sc rows = 4 inches

Take time to check gauge.

PATTERN NOTES
Weave in ends as work progresses.

Join with slip stitch as indicated unless otherwise stated.

Leave a 6-inch end or length specified when fastening off yarn.

Each row is worked on right side.

Each row is worked carrying unused color across wrong side. Solid color rows have a 2nd strand of same color carried on wrong side.

If you are right-handed, read every row of chart from right to left.

If you are left-handed, read every row of chart from left to right.

SHAWL

Row 1: With Caribbean sea, ch 49, sc in 2nd ch from hook, sc in each rem ch across, turn. *(48 sc)*

Row 2: Ch 1, sc in each sc across, turn.

Rows 3–300: Rep row 2. At end of last row, fasten off.

POCKET
MAKE 2.

Row 1: With Caribbean sea and leaving a 3-inch end, ch 35, **carrying a 2nd strand of Caribbean sea underneath** *(see Pattern Notes)*, working in **back lps** *(see Stitch Guide)*, sc in 2nd ch from hook, sc in each rem ch across. Leaving a 3-inch end of both yarns, fasten off.

Note: For following rows, follow chart for color changes and work in back lps.

Row 2: Make slip knot on hook and join yarn with sc in first sc, sc in each rem sc across. Fasten off.

Rows 3–32: Rep row 2.

BORDER
Row 1: With RS facing and last row at top, **join** *(see Pattern Notes)* Caribbean sea in end of last row at left-hand edge, working across side in ends of rows, sc in each row across, working across foundation ch, 3 sc in first ch, sc in each ch across to last ch, 3 sc in last ch, working across next side in ends of rows, sc in each row across to last row, turn.

Row 2: Ch 1, sc in each sc across, working 3 sc in 2nd sc of each 3-sc group, turn.

Row 3: Ch 1, sc in each sc across, working 3 sc in 2nd sc of each 3-sc group. Fasten off.

Trim ends to just short of Border.

FINISHING
Referring to photo for placement, sew Pockets on Shawl. ∎

COLOR KEY
■ Caribbean sea
■ Fire red
■ Nectarine
□ White ash
■ Natural

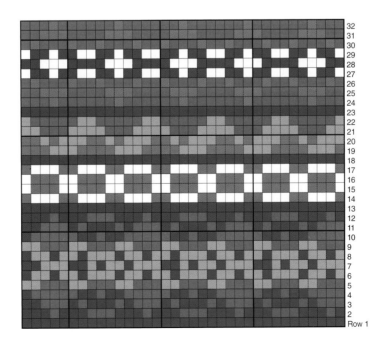

Shawl
Chart

Hat & Scarf

HAT

SKILL LEVEL

EASY

FINISHED SIZE

Fits 18–21-inch head circumference

MATERIALS

- Universal Yarn Deluxe Worsted medium (worsted) weight yarn (3½ oz/220 yds/100g per skein): 1 skein #41141 roasted almond
- Universal Yarn Classic Worsted medium (worsted) weight yarn (3½ oz/197 yds/ 100g per skein): 1 skein each #7116 fiesta and #7087 linden green
- Size G/6/4mm crochet hook or size needed to obtain gauge
- Tapestry needle

GAUGE

12 sc and 12 sc rows = 4 inches

Take time to check gauge.

PATTERN NOTES

Weave in ends as work progresses.

Join with slip stitch as indicated unless otherwise stated.

Body of Hat is worked in continuous rounds. Do not join unless specified; mark beginning of round.

Each round is worked carrying unused color across wrong side. Solid color rounds have a 2nd strand of same color carried on wrong side.

If you are right-handed, read every row of chart from right to left.

If you are left-handed, read every row of chart from left to right.

HAT
BODY

Rnd 1: With roasted almond, ch 72 loosely, **join** *(see Pattern Notes)* in first ch to form a ring, ch 1, **carrying a strand of roasted almonds on WS** *(see Pattern Notes)* and working in **back lps** *(see Stitch Guide)*, sc in each ch across. Do not join. *(72 sc)*

Note: Place st marker in first st of rnd, moving up as work progresses.

Rnds 2–6: Working in back lps, sc in each sc around.

Note: For following rnds, follow chart for color changes and work in back lps.

Rnds 7–21: Sc in each sc around.

Note: For following rnds, work with roasted almond only, carrying 2nd strand on WS and work in back lps.

Rnd 22: Sc in each sc around.

Rnd 23: *Sc in each of next 4 sc, **sc dec** *(see Stitch Guide)* in next 2 sc, rep from * 11 times. *(60 sc)*

Rnd 24: *Sc in each of next 3 sc, sc dec in next 2 sc, rep from * 11 times. *(48 sc)*

Rnd 25: *Sc in each of next 2 sc, sc dec in next 2 sc, rep from * 11 times. *(36 sc)*

Rnd 26: *Sc in next sc, sc dec in next 2 sc, rep from * 11 times. *(24 sc)*

Rnd 27: [Sc dec in next 2 sc] 12 times. Fasten off. *(12 sc)*

FIRST EAR FLAP

Row 1: With RS facing and foundation ch at top, make slip knot on hook and join roasted almond with sc in any ch, sc in each of next 14 chs, leaving rem chs unworked, turn. *(15 sc)*

Row 2: Ch 1, sc in each sc across, turn.

Row 3: Ch 1, sc in first sc, sc dec in next 2 sc, sc in each sc across to last 3 sc, sc dec in next 2 sc, sc in last sc, turn. *(13 sc)*

Row 4: Ch 1, sc in each sc across, turn.

Rows 5–24: [Rep rows 2 and 3 alternately] 10 times. At end of last row, fasten off.

2ND EAR FLAP

Row 1: Sk next 21 chs from First Ear Flap, make slip knot on hook and join roasted almond with sc in next ch, sc in each of next 14 chs, leaving rem chs unworked, turn. *(15 sc)*

Rows 2–24: Rep rows 2–24 of First Ear Flap.

EDGING

Make slip knot on hook and join linden green with sc in any unworked ch of foundation ch, *sc in each rem unworked ch, sc up side of next Ear Flap, 3 sc in center top of Ear Flap, sc down Ear Flap, rep from * once, join in beg sc. Fasten off.

BRAIDS

For each side, cut 12 (48-inch) strands of yarn. Draw through point of ear flap. Divide into three 8-strand sections and braid to desired length. Knot and trim ends.

SCARF

SKILL LEVEL

EASY

FINISHED SIZE

5 inches wide x 60 inches long including fringe

MATERIALS

- Universal Yarn Deluxe Worsted medium (worsted) weight yarn (3½ oz/220 yds/100g per skein):
    2 skeins #41141 roasted almond
- Universal Yarn Classic Worsted medium (worsted) weight yarn (3½ oz/197 yds/100g per skein):
    1 skein each #7116 fiesta and #7087 linden green
- Size G/6/4mm crochet hook or size needed to obtain gauge
- Tapestry needle

GAUGE

18 sc and 16 sc rows = 4 inches

Take time to check gauge.

PATTERN NOTES

Weave in ends as work progresses.

Leave an 8–10-inch end at either end for fringe.

Each row is worked carrying unused color across wrong side. Solid color rows have a 2nd strand of same color carried on wrong side.

If you are right-handed, read every row of chart from right to left.

If you are left-handed, read every row of chart from left to right.

SCARF

Row 1: With roasted almond, ch 234. Fasten off. **Carrying 2nd strand of roasted almond across WS** (*see Pattern Notes*) and working in **back lps** (*see Stitch Guide*), make slip knot on hook and join roasted almond with sc in first ch, sc in each rem ch across. Fasten off. *(234 sc)*

Note: For following rows, follow chart for color changes and work in back lps.

Row 2: Make slip knot on hook and join yarn with sc in first sc, sc in each rem sc across, fasten off.

Rows 3–19: Rep row 2. ■

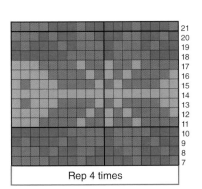

Hat
Chart

COLOR KEY
■ Roasted almond
■ Linden green
■ Fiesta

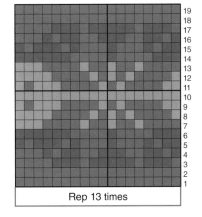

Scarf
Chart

Purse

SKILL LEVEL

EASY

FINISHED SIZE
12½ inches wide x 13½ inches tall (size may vary due to felting)

MATERIALS
- Universal Yarn Deluxe Worsted medium (worsted) weight wool yarn (3½ oz/220 yds/100g per skein):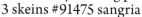
    3 skeins #91475 sangria
    1 skein each #41141 roasted almond, #3608 marigold and #12256 tangerine flash
- Size O/12mm crochet hook or size needed to obtain gauge
- Tapestry needle
- Stitch marker

GAUGE
8 sc and 8 sc rows = 4 inches

Take time to check gauge.

PATTERN NOTES
Leave a 6-inch end when fastening off yarn.

Each round is worked carrying unused color across wrong side. Solid color rounds have a 2nd strand of same color carried on wrong side.

If you are right-handed, read every row of chart from right to left.

If you are left-handed, read every row of chart from left to right.

PURSE
BOTTOM
Row 1: With sangria, ch 11, sc in 2nd ch from hook, sc in each rem ch across, turn. *(10 sc)*

Row 2: Ch 1, sc in each sc across, turn.

Rows 3–36: Rep row 2.

BODY
Note: Body is worked in continuous rnds. Do not join unless specified; mark beg of rnd.

Rnd 37: Ch 1, 3 sc in first sc, sc in each of next 8 sc, 3 sc in last sc, working across next side in ends of rows, work 35 sc evenly sp across, working across next side in chs of foundation ch, 3 sc in first ch, sc in each of next 8 chs, 3 sc in last ch, working across next side in ends of rows, work 35 sc across. Do not join. *(98 sc)*

Rnd 38: Sc in each sc around.

Rnds 39–51: Rep rnd 38.

Note: For rnds 52–60, follow chart for color changes and work in back lps.

Rnds 52–60: Rep rnd 38.

Rnds 61–72: With sangria, rep rnd 38.

HANDLES
Rnd 73: Sc in each of next 36 sc, ch 15, sk next 15 sc, sc in each of next 34 sc, ch 15, sk next 15 sc, sc in next sc. *(68 sc, 2 ch-15 sps)*

Rnd 74: Sc in each sc and in each ch around. *(98 sc)*

Rnds 75–79: Rep rnd 38. At end of last rnd, join with sl st in beg sc. Fasten off.

FINISHING
To felt Purse, do not weave in ends. Place Purse in nylon mesh bag or a pillow case.

Set wash temperature to "Hot," and the load size to "Small," with high agitation. Add the rinse-free soap, if you choose. (One tablespoon is usually enough.)

Add an old pair of jeans or tennis ball to help increase agitation.

Start washer and set timer. Check progress of felting every 5 minutes or so. In a front-load washer, use "Pause" or "Stop" button, and wait for water level to settle and door latch to open. If your front-load washer does not have this feature, it is almost impossible to felt correctly.

Keep checking Purse until it has reached the firm, felted stage. You may have to take the piece out of the washer, wring it out and see how it is doing. Continue this process as many times as necessary to reach the final felted stage. Do not allow washer to rinse and spin, as this will stop felting process, and it can add permanent creases to felted piece.

Rinse Purse in cool to warm water. If a rinse-free wool wash is used, this is not needed.

For some shaping, use towels or some sort of form inside Purse to shape, otherwise dry flat.

It may take several days to dry, so be patient! ∎

COLOR KEY
■ Sangria
■ Roasted almond
□ Marigold
■ Tangerine flash

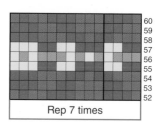

Rep 7 times

Purse
Chart

STITCH GUIDE

FOR MORE COMPLETE INFORMATION,
VISIT **ANNIESCATALOG.COM/STITCHGUIDE**

STITCH ABBREVIATIONS

beg ....begin/begins/beginning
bpdc .... back post double crochet
bpsc ....back post single crochet
bptr ....back post treble crochet
CC.. contrasting color
ch(s) ....chain(s)
ch- ....refers to chain or space
    previously made (i.e., ch-1 space)
ch sp(s) .... chain space(s)
cl(s) ....cluster(s)
cm .... centimeter(s)
dc.........................double crochet (singular/plural)
dc dec .... double crochet 2 or more
    stitches together, as indicated
dec.............................. decrease/decreases/decreasing
dtr .... double treble crochet
ext ....extended
fpdc.............................. front post double crochet
fpsc ....front post single crochet
fptr ....front post treble crochet
g ....gram(s)
hdc .... half double crochet
hdc dec ....half double crochet 2 or more
    stitches together, as indicated
inc .... increase/increases/increasing
lp(s) ....loop(s)
MC ....main color
mm ....millimeter(s)
oz ....ounce(s)
pc ....popcorn(s)
rem ....remain/remains/remaining
rep(s) ....repeat(s)
rnd(s) ....round(s)
RS ....right side
sc .... single crochet (singular/plural)
sc dec ....single crochet 2 or more
    stitches together, as indicated
sk ....skip/skipped/skipping
sl st(s) .... slip stitch(es)
sp(s) .... space(s)/spaced
st(s) ....stitch(es)
tog...together
tr ....treble crochet
trtr ....triple treble
WS .... wrong side
yd(s) ....yard(s)
yo .... yarn over

YARN CONVERSION

OUNCES TO GRAMS	GRAMS TO OUNCES
1 .... 28.4	25 .... ⅞
2 .... 56.7	40 .... 1⅔
3 .... 85.0	50 .... 1¾
4 .... 113.4	100 .... 3½

UNITED STATES		UNITED KINGDOM
sl st (slip stitch)	=	sc (single crochet)
sc (single crochet)	=	dc (double crochet)
hdc (half double crochet)	=	htr (half treble crochet)
dc (double crochet)	=	tr (treble crochet)
tr (treble crochet)	=	dtr (double treble crochet)
dtr (double treble crochet)	=	ttr (triple treble crochet)
skip	=	miss

Reverse single crochet (reverse sc): Ch 1, sk first st, working from left to right, insert hook in next st from front to back, draw up lp on hook, yo, and draw through both lps on hook.

Chain (ch): Yo, pull through lp on hook.

Single crochet (sc): Insert hook in st, yo, pull through st, yo, pull through both lps on hook.

Double crochet (dc): Yo, insert hook in st, yo, pull through st, [yo, pull through 2 lps] twice.

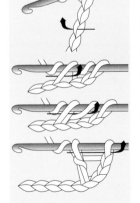

Front loop (front lp) Back loop (back lp)

Front Loop   Back Loop

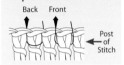

Front post stitch (fp): Back post stitch (bp): When working post st, insert hook from right to left around post of st on previous row.

Back   Front

Post of Stitch

Half double crochet (hdc): Yo, insert hook in st, yo, pull through st, yo, pull through all 3 lps on hook.

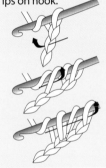

Double treble crochet (dtr): Yo 3 times, insert hook in st, yo, pull through st, [yo, pull through 2 lps] 4 times.

Slip stitch (sl st): Insert hook in st, pull through both lps on hook.

Chain color change (ch color change) Yo with new color, draw through last lp on hook.

Double crochet color change (dc color change) Drop first color, yo with new color, draw through last 2 lps of st.

Treble crochet (tr): Yo twice, insert hook in st, yo, pull through st, [yo, pull through 2 lps] 3 times.

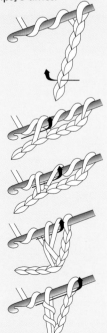

Single crochet decrease (sc dec): (Insert hook, yo, draw lp through) in each of the sts indicated, yo, draw through all lps on hook.

Example of 2-sc dec

Half double crochet decrease (hdc dec): (Yo, insert hook, yo, draw lp through) in each of the sts indicated, yo, draw through all lps on hook.

Example of 2-hdc dec

Double crochet decrease (dc dec): (Yo, insert hook, yo, draw lp through, yo, draw through 2 lps on hook) in each of the sts indicated, yo, draw through all lps on hook.

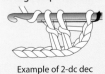

Example of 2-dc dec

Treble crochet decrease (tr dec): Holding back last lp of each st, tr in each of the sts indicated, yo, pull through all lps on hook.

Example of 2-tr dec

Metric
Conversion
Charts

METRIC CONVERSIONS				
yards	x	.9144	=	metres (m)
yards	x	91.44	=	centimetres (cm)
inches	x	2.54	=	centimetres (cm)
inches	x	25.40	=	millimetres (mm)
inches	x	.0254	=	metres (m)

centimetres	x	.3937	=	inches
metres	x	1.0936	=	yards

INCHES INTO MILLIMETRES & CENTIMETRES (Rounded off slightly)

inches	mm	cm	inches	cm	inches	cm	inches	cm
1/8	3	0.3	5	12.5	21	53.5	38	96.5
1/4	6	0.6	5 1/2	14	22	56	39	99
3/8	10	1	6	15	23	58.5	40	101.5
1/2	13	1.3	7	18	24	61	41	104
5/8	15	1.5	8	20.5	25	63.5	42	106.5
3/4	20	2	9	23	26	66	43	109
7/8	22	2.2	10	25.5	27	68.5	44	112
1	25	2.5	11	28	28	71	45	114.5
1 1/4	32	3.2	12	30.5	29	73.5	46	117
1 1/2	38	3.8	13	33	30	76	47	119.5
1 3/4	45	4.5	14	35.5	31	79	48	122
2	50	5	15	38	32	81.5	49	124.5
2 1/2	65	6.5	16	40.5	33	84	50	127
3	75	7.5	17	43	34	86.5		
3 1/2	90	9	18	46	35	89		
4	100	10	19	48.5	36	91.5		
4 1/2	115	11.5	20	51	37	94		

KNITTING NEEDLES CONVERSION CHART

Canada/U.S.	0	1	2	3	4	5	6	7	8	9	10	10½	11	13	15
Metric (mm)	2	2¼	2¾	3¼	3½	3¾	4	4½	5	5½	6	6½	8	9	10

CROCHET HOOKS CONVERSION CHART

Canada/U.S.	1/B	2/C	3/D	4/E	5/F	6/G	8/H	9/I	10/J	10½/K	N
Metric (mm)	2.25	2.75	3.25	3.5	3.75	4.25	5	5.5	6	6.5	9.0

Annie's™ *Learn to Fair Isle Crochet* is published by Annie's, 306 East Parr Road, Berne, IN 46711. Printed in USA. Copyright © 2012 Annie's. All rights reserved. This publication may not be reproduced in part or in whole without written permission from the publisher.

RETAIL STORES: If you would like to carry this pattern book or any other Annie's publications, visit AnniesWSL.com

Every effort has been made to ensure that the instructions in this pattern book are complete and accurate. We cannot, however, take responsibility for human error, typographical mistakes or variations in individual work. Please visit AnniesCustomerCare.com to check for pattern updates.

ISBN: 978-1-59635-714-3

1 2 3 4 5 6 7 8 9